QUICK
QUESTION

An Imprint of HarperCollins*Publishers*

JOHN ASHBERY

NEW POEMS

QUICK QUESTION. COPYRIGHT © 2012 BY JOHN ASHBERY. ALL RIGHTS RESERVED. PRINTED IN THE UNITED STATES OF AMERICA. NO PART OF THIS BOOK MAY BE USED OR REPRODUCED IN ANY MANNER WHATSOEVER WITHOUT WRITTEN PERMISSION EXCEPT IN THE CASE OF BRIEF QUOTATIONS EMBODIED IN CRITICAL ARTICLES AND REVIEWS. FOR INFORMATION ADDRESS HARPERCOLLINS PUBLISHERS, 10 EAST 53RD STREET, NEW YORK, NY 10022. / HARPERCOLLINS BOOKS MAY BE PURCHASED FOR EDUCATIONAL, BUSINESS, OR SALES PROMOTIONAL USE. FOR INFORMATION PLEASE WRITE: SPECIAL MARKETS DEPARTMENT, HARPERCOLLINS PUBLISHERS, 10 EAST 53RD STREET, NEW YORK, NY 10022. / FIRST EDITION / PRINTED ON ACID-FREE PAPER / DESIGNED BY QUEMADURA / LIBRARY OF CONGRESS CATALOGING-IN-PUBLICATION DATA HAS BEEN APPLIED FOR. / ISBN 978-0-06-222595-5 / 12 13 14 15 16 QK/RRD 10 9 8 7 6 5 4 3 2 1

FOR JANE FREILICHER

WORDS TO
THAT EFFECT

The drive down was smooth
but after we arrived things started to go haywire,
first one thing and then another. The days
scudded past like tumbleweed, slow then fast,
then slow again. The sky was sweet and plain.
You remember how still it was then,
a season putting its arms into a coat and staying unwrapped
for a long, a little time.

It was during the week we talked about deforestation.
How sad that everything has to change,
yet what a relief, too! Otherwise we'd only have
looking forward to look forward to.
The moment would be a bud
that never filled, only persevered
in a static trance, before it came to be no more.

We'd walked a little way in our shoes.
I was sure you'd remember how it had been

the other time, before the messenger came to your door
and seemed to want to peer in and size up the place.
So each evening became a forbidden morning
of thunder and curdled milk, though the invoices
got forwarded and birds settled on the periphery.

QUICK QUESTION

Here in the museum we do not invite trouble,
only establishment woes, sort of. We can bet farther
and classier with no returns. Sometimes late at night

cars droned and paled: Splurge and repent—
wasn't that the idea? It was your initiative
that brought us here, through the difficult part

of a city. Some angels
seemed to teeter on the wooden fence.
Were we all they knew?

Or are we part of their mind-cleansing
ritual, necessary and discardable?
Doesn't that make more sense?

Less than an hour before our return from the lake
trees blossomed like shells exploding,
the landscape sucked in its breath,

taking its time as always.
I meant to speak to your mother about it,
but never forgave her for not being here, and drab,

the way mothers are supposed to be,
I think. Too many applications of the rule ensue.
There are too many, always with us

under the tree that stands on the lawn
but is no longer there, as if to prove it was a dream,
a different time slot.

THE SHORT ANSWER

I am forced to sleepwalk much of the time.
We hold on to these old ways, are troubled
sometimes and then the geyser goes away,
time gutted. In and of itself there is
no great roar, force pitted against force that
makes up in time what it loses in speed.
The waterfalls, the canyon, a royal I-told-you-so
comes back to greet us at the beginning.
How was your trip? Oh I didn't last
you see, folded over like the margin
of a dream of the thing-in-itself. Well, and
what have we come to? A paper-thin past,
just so, and 'tis pity. We regurgitate
old anthems and what has come to pass, and why
dwell on these. Why make things more difficult
than they already are? Because if it's boring
in a different way, that'll be interesting too.
That's what I say.

That rascal, he jumped over the fence.
I'm wiping my pince-nez now. Did you ever hear from
the one who said he'd be back once it was over,

who eluded me even in my sleep? That was a particularly
promising time, we thought. Now the sun's out
and it's raining again. Just like a day from
the compendium. I'll vouch for you,
and we can go on scrolling as though nothing had risen,
the horizon forest looks back at us. The preacher
shook his head, the evangelist balanced two spools
at the end of his little makeshift rope. We'd gone too far.
We'd have to come back in a day or so.

CROSS ISLAND

You've probably done this already
and if not, where's the sympathy?
Scratched the frozen surface one time
too many, pulled away from the mirror
like a tractor-trailer backing up
in a snowstorm, to let the inevitable bar
fall into place, seeking solace somewhere,
clanging. We've all pointed to similar occurrences:
the person's melodious rage, talking back
on the phone. If you don't hurry
to the city harsh words will develop
on your screen.
                    All of us whistling
for the best, like you, hawking sweetness,
hope the blessing will be for now.
Really, who can say? There was a hero once
who carved these parts. No one can remember
what his greeting was, whether he came to inter
an older one, or set the chain in motion
again. No one knew him. But when laughter
erupts on the adjacent floor, it is as though
we understood. Once. Like you already said,

finders are keepers only for a time.
Time marches on. Depart misery.
He was moved through it as though
by configurations of the crowd who came
to need us. Thank you for being with us.

THE ALLEGATIONS

I'm here to say we didn't rule out nepotism,
or kindness. To others than you the sky is flat
as flypaper over Texas, some parts receding
faster than others. A lecture out of control.

I heard the same thing coming up,
decided there was some kind of weirdness
on the back burner. Oh it's OK, actually, I'm,
well, maybe not shocked, but a little serious
this time. We paid our dues, fetched some concern
for the allegations. I'd like to hear about those.
Well, you would. The check was duly deposited
in the wrong bank. Everything seemed fine
if adjacent to one's main preoccupation:
If one of those bottles should happen to fall!

With these popular machines it always accretes
in a way to distinguish one. No thanks.
I heard the same thing coming up:
A really helpful hotel bandit stopped me
on the stair, the staff having already fled.

The reaction shot was a no-brainer. Try to feel your ear,
you'll see. The music continues to unroll
in the empty corridor. Why we sold the porch
is another ending. We're all at odds here.
It'll come true for you in Kansas City, Iowa.

REST AREA

The word is lectern it lacks
embarrassment or something but
then you too knew like through
a stocking. Other outriders told how
in those days quite a lot got through.
Others fainted ("on the sidelines")
while still others congratulated
their neighbors on their luck
(must have been a shock
to learn the counterfeiters were
plain citizens after all like
everybody). And still they come
to pick up after them and there
is nothing on the margin except hairs.
Nobody could imagine how it counts
against you yet supports when least
imaginable and the climate
installs a blur due to hooliganism.
Meanwhile the breath of morning shreds
a chill that was ours and otherwise
installed we knew to sign off
on the élan and faint for the departed

just as everybody knew it would
and nobody left any wiser.
This would be all for the time
being the shutters closing
for after all it was time
and we can't tell how much
any of us knows or knew at
any time in the past or recent
past. That as they say is the puzzle
the great total that touches your plate
as the siren goes off kissing the child
on the shoulder and tanks retreat
as though the war was never meant
and none of us were supposed to die as
we in fact weren't.

RECENT HISTORY

Desperate asks, how driven batty
by climate change, can we not make out
a stranger's silhouette in the dooryard?
How can I lick some calendars where somnolent
shepherds bear witness while porcelain
nymphs conjugate somebody else's
irregular verb? I'm still not in anti-personnel
mode, yet that gigolo's DNA is all over
the doorposts, from mudroom to powder room.

They were early, as usual. Can't you guys ever
be late, we wondered, though one wouldn't
necessarily want that either. Arriving in one piece,
jaded, is enough for some. Not to be slimed
by the lake, or weather, or accounted for
by the bruising wind may be all it needs
to recover from a weekend's erosion. If you take into
consideration the snobbery that lets us breathe happily in pairs
for sure we'll have traversed a veranda's worth
of elegies, or epics. Let it mean something.

You mean in other ways that changed our lives?
Somethin' o' that, I says. Is that why clouds

withered scrappily and no tune finally approved
its margins? Fringed with decay all along,
it was, and if who knew better than our selves' somber
asides they wouldn't bet on it. But I was a
child here for a long time. I even learned to read
by the glare from that mud factory, fumed
and hectored hostile witnesses, and so
sailed down with evening to be done with penances,
haphazard scraps of truth on beauty's trash heap.
I'd do it again in a moment, offered the chance,
but luck seldom cometh our way twice,
ye gods! We serve two masters: haddock and bream,
while crumbs muster stingily at our lips.
It was a day like any other, torn from the register.

A VOICE FROM
THE FIREPLACE

Like a windup denture in a joke store
fate approaches, leans quietly. Let's see . . .
There was moreover meaning in the last clause,
meaning we couldn't equate
from what was happening to us down the block.
We approached with some hesitancy:
Let "I dare not" wait upon "I would."
Wasn't it April? Weren't things more likely to last
in this or any season? Rhymes we like.
More than rhythm, they provide a life preserver
for embarrassing sorties. Um, some day we'll be grown up too,
the desk lights not cancel the barge
as it approaches the corner of avenues.

Well, we
sweated that out. It amounts to self-importance.
Whether the sea is a vernacular one
only heroes can describe. Why don't you pluck me one?
Seems they all rushed to the other side
of the deck, causing alarm.

Wind shriveled the rags that were left.
Hold on a minute, we'll get you aloft.
No sense taking up time with vellum sunsets,
he hears, and cannot stay. The whitish, gluey smell
of the forest imbibes our earnings in a dream.
Egg whites dry at room temperature.

In my mature moments I was robotic like you
but never canceled my interest.
We all attempt starting out, yet few undergo
the first few days of orientation lightly.
Which is funny, I mean with so many around to project
enlightenment or entertainment. If you live
in a wren house you'll quickly understand what I mean.

That, needless to say, was the last time
I heard from them. I continue to get their flyers
in the mail but the project remains uninhabited.
Flowers and goats cram the entrance with something
you can see over. The orange sea propels itself
lightly forward, ever in quest of spectators,
but you can only do just so much in the way of self-formation.
I hadn't expected it to be otherwise,
yet it doesn't seem right. Neither is it unjust,
only pro forma. Nights imply seasons
and much in the way of impish narrative, while in daylight
it's a matter of getting flush with the pavement.

Don't forget to check every box
on the front door and leave change for the milkman.
Too bad they spotted us. Like I say,
no jury will ever convict he or I. Off you go then.
An egg is a puzzle, a tree a piece of that puzzle.
I've had a pleasant but uneven time.
My helpmates could aver as much. Let us know
how much we owe you. The balloon is ascending
above ferns, teacup chimneys, striped stockings.
So long training wheels. I'm gone for three weeks at a time.

IN DREAMS I KISS
YOUR HAND, MADAME

Like those feelings we can never throw out.
He would be tired, or outraged,
never satisfied to light on a peak
in a distant mountain range.
Like dreaming, but not enough.

Which reminds me that I dreamed I was walking
on stilts, last night. A little girl
gave them to me, and said it was easy
to walk on them, which it wasn't, though
it wasn't too difficult either,
just a little scary. I wore long pants
that covered the stilts, and was surprised
that no one thought I was any taller,
or almost no one. But I soon forgot
about them as did the people around me,
like the mannequins often seen
in store windows, though not so much anymore.

THE NEW CROWD

Fifteen minutes is all they give you.

Who could whip up an omelet in that amount of time,
let alone a memoir of the *ancien régime,* beloved era?
That kind of concentration of the language comes along
once in a lifetime, or so they say. I'm not opining.
And I drive the plate down the stairs . . .

Fifteen-cent poems, pretty good in jail.
His ancestors are across the street
if someone asks. We dreamed of you for a decade.
Pretty strong stuff. More stories came along,
none knew where. They found a new recipe for sangria
lacking the plainness of the old, finding little to replace it with.
The hurricane season swept us along, inhabiting
far too many pictures. Is it always like this,

the little girl wanted to know? Well, yes and no.
Some of them seem to like it, they keep
coming back like a song, and you're easily pleased
without accuracy. Once the sun has set it's

all the same, one is in or out. By most accounted
a success, it stained the leggings of many a drifter.
In sight of apiaries at 25 after the hour, remember
the style of mercy, the red-hearted, country level
residential area. Hey, cliffdwellers!

IN A LONELY PLACE

Dry-eyed from weeping I consent
to the stratagems that brought us here:
what collins, cooler, Cuba libre,
grasshopper, gin sling, brandy alexander,
Manhattan, martini, Moscow mule,
whatever sounded lush along the way.
Acquiescence yet breeds demurral in its wake—
uh-huh, un-hunh, um-hum,
yes sirree, why yes, *mais si*,
indeed, indeedy, righto, rather! The average
lighthouse is mostly ancient by now
and would just have to get up anyway
if anybody'd let it. Rescuers divvied up
the proceeds and it all ended
on a positive note with crashing cymbals
and jingling psalteries. Satisfactorily, in a word.

Yet what of other nights still unplotted?
Strictly speaking we ignore these
till it's no longer possible, by which time
something will have been worked out. Some chapter heading
to alert authorities to our amusing plight.

I told you all would become supple,
with large, clear type and purposeful
vignettes. Not the kind to take one's mind off
the brewing storm, sidling now here,
now there, like punch or piña colada.

MORE RELUCTANT

It's time for a little chamber music
of Arensky or Borodin, something minor
and enduring, as we imagine ourselves
to be, let that be a wake-up call,
as the man said. When you turned I thought
you've got to stop me, I'm out of control
but mature, so every step I take
counts. Meanwhile you were rambling on
about something, nobody knows what,
so that behind the wall of the setting sun
the great presences could collect and mutate
as in former times. Wasn't it all a legend
or fictive construction? Why did we
think it mattered for us and not for others?
The whole urban chaos spalls and before
we know it the subject has changed.
What other conversation are you in?
Whose day has spent?

                          Working in the town,
that lummox was charged with evaluation,
so if groups of young people started off
in an opposite direction there would be a mention

sometimes. The housefronts seem more gaudy this year,
eggshell and pale green and no one
wants to take the responsibility. Moonlighters
observe customs of the spruce of the year
the way tin warriors would keep company with paper
models if others left the square unsupervised.
By the way they have a store in Hartford,
Connecticut. I often pee sometimes.
The awful leaf was congruent,
too. Mothers and hustlers bridled in the choking
dust that afflicts it from everywhere, yet owns
to no thread in the proceedings. They washed
it clean every night. In the mornings the footprints
were back, but no one was wiser. A little
bunny or some kind of ferret was probably
there too, and bore witness as only rodents can.
I could see the guy. Some in lesser hands
say repeatedly, wash it out, the shared indictment
ought to stand if only so they can all go home. Wonderful,
that it is. Now that wasn't so easy, was it?

UNLIKE THE CAMELOPARD

It can't be anything too obvious, like a procession
of cars that doesn't know it's a procession,
or a paint job among many that's rented
from a theatrical properties company.
Yet it must realize itself, or turn stodgy
in one afternoon. They want so hard to be American,
but in the end it's where you come from that counts,
not who you are or who you were going to be.

Unlike the camelopard it can't be anything too obvious
or unfamiliar. To just stay lowered, and gradually
the watermark will reappear, sorrow shaking in the trees,
images and the like, bashful demagogues come to congratulate us,
moving us imperceptibly closer to the goalposts,
approved by the Rake's Progress Administration, chasing
the sap lest it harden into gunk and deplete us,
means that anything couldn't have happened.

So strange signs are going to appear.
Longtime he sat upon the porch.
Ten billion times the resolution dipped, waved
and was off. Happy weather! Exactly.

RESISTING ARREST

A year and a day later the wolf stopped
by as planned. He made conversation
about this and that but you could tell
from the way he favored his gums that all was
not well. Later the driving pool shifted.
I had no idea that you were planning
to stage an operation but it's all right
this time. Then I read your account and
was dully impressed, right at the edge
of the sea where the land asserts itself.

He told a cheering crowd the infighting was over
at least for that day. They had more affairs
to remember than just that one time. Why,
he went over it and that was that. Plethoras
to be announced, etc. You're telling me.

Warming to his theme he brought us in
as though we belonged. Ma and I
decided to wait it out but here again
he was unyielding, hoping to lure a big-name
retailer on the strength of our fevered gain

over the past months of quasi activity,
dark with relative distress. That proved uncertain
and doesn't smash it all. They liked what they heard.

No one wanted to shoulder responsibility
for the times and to slog off to uncertain
destinies in fiberglass pilot houses.
I had no idea that you meant it to be early.
The fatal tarnish of the everyday
groans and incites mobs to splendor
and wrongdoing as though a tissue of sleeping-cars
were to upbraid dawn. They asked me to read
off a result or temper a calamity like I was involved
in the unfolding reaction with everything
else, they wanted me to reside at 478 Pavilion Avenue
and the story would resolve itself munificently.

Not in my receding horsepital. I paid
my dues to the city and look
how out on a limb I am and you could guess
this too, you could plan more strategically.
That's all for now kid. Drop me a line sometime,
seriously.

WHO WERE
THOSE PEOPLE

He was down there
sitting on that.
Why is dumbness to be prized?
If it's not anybody's favorite
who said that?

Here are the financial reports
like a lovesick champignon.
She is missing a dungeon,
to pay from flooding.

It's all terribly charming,
night, reiterated.
Privately one suspected
a housekeeper. Wyoming
and West Virginia lead the country
in chewing tobacco consumption.
But you knew that.

DOUBLE WHOOPEE

As I was saying it's a never-ending getting
closer if you will, a class-unconsciousness searing
these ears for a lifetime, and by then it's time
to wonder again why you undertook a reckoning
so near the end. A distant polka assaults;
this time around there's a valid reason for illegal
punchdrunk after-hours festooning. Just as, I
reasoned, as you with me, we all finished
out on the flats. The tide! The one thing we forgot.

Which is why in these late days a basement runaround
procures the shucks earlier arbiters cautioned against
and night's surprising arrival turned fears to ghosts.
There are times a barrel organ sounds sharp
and sweet as all musical expectancy. Can be seen as
coming round again, nothing at all the matter with it.
The next day's silhouette on a screen even seems reassuring,
the lack of stuffing a refreshment. So when gazes cancel
each other and rabbits go hopping away it's the birds
are seen to withdraw after that, the "nest" symbol
mysteriously unavailable. You who puked
at the sight of a hairnet, where's your gimcrack lesson now?

Why else fidget so close
to the heart of things, the hoary corporate logo that defines
our monstrosity for some, pulling the tide toward the horizon
like a bedspread? Indeed why let being populous
concern us at all? Unless we too secretly shift
deeper into the room as tale telling starts, worrier,
you understand?

Interesting to ask so unevenly. The master doesn't take my calls.
We mustn't overdo listening pretty,
jogging the thunderstorm equipment to live in peace.
Anybody not having any?

LIKE ANY LEAVES

They said the birds didn't do any damage.
The life we row to the uneasy center,
mosquito by mosquito, loses the forest.

But that was a different tower. It won't fold
or digress. As confusing as a slap on the arm,
runners loop back to the confessional.

THE COST OF SLEEP

Jarred by thought's boomerang you waken
on an open hillside. This is what it means
to be opposed, alert. A tray of lead curios
at his side means not to interrupt, but
as so often leaves its vines in dust
where students can ransom them. Here, this
is what I meant. Like shoe-pretty.

Apparently that's how they measure them,
cats in their underwear, as though nothing
before had mattered and never will. I'm sure others
have had these ideas; nay, too many.
Others tomorrow will want to sign on again
for the full bill of goods. It's not
as often as you think earth turns, round
cheek up against the casement we thought was nowhere.

Now I'm in on it. Go in peace lest
they signal you I was here, telling my beads,
for we were forewarned and by the same

token are involved in my body institute.
He came up and was laughing. Your friendly
neighborhood diaspora withstood a winter of puns
a likely bloke had sidetracked,
just the two of us. Let's stick it out.

ABSENT AGENDA

To be old only along the sea
isn't a bad idea. One is turned
into another kind of extremist.
The weather gets to you. When it's wet
you stay indoors. "Plangent" is viable.
One turns to one in tears, the sky shaking
visibly.

Why are you crying?
I know it's none of my business, but . . .
The long haul intrudes, involves us
later on. Dreams are weeded
for their own good, and the plant grows
in darkness. Earth is tilted,
better farther along. The whole time around
salesmen in weathered suits confirm the background,
only on business. Can you believe it,
he quoted his "mistress." Told us
we'd be having our own moment
once the people and things gave their caution.

Invariably the fabric is chafed,
the wood aisles feathery to the touch

as though autumn had fallen off the truck again.
Are these animals to be prized for their musk
or will the kids imbibe us, recognizing each
toy as a distinction, something to be shelved
and consulted when distracted, at some kind of grand
occasion or event no one recognizes anymore?

UNFIT TO STAND TRIAL

A beautiful debut comes to mind:
new smells, new songs, strands too tightly wound,
music—rhythms more secure, glancing harmonies.
They're pharmacies.

I can't eat them any greener.
Each passing bird mopes, then shivers
at the concussion of all the things we've created,
and which you had something to do with.

And then again right after,
opinions get stored away. It's eight o'clock at night
with fire engines and an impromptu softball game.
Why do these templates trail me the way they do?

Not so someone would remember,
the lie dies hard, so that we're in it.
We don't deserve our impressions
but are convicted anyway. Most come loose.

Snails weave glittering topaz trails
along the driveway.
You promised me to come early with the antidote.
Like two children in love we take it anyway.

HOW I MET YOU

I'd had a "good night's sleep," meaning
thinking of waking, and waking,
shifting closer together, and then not.
That and the music we're getting, sometimes
timely, sometimes incomplete, like Ulysses and Penelope
talking it over in a back room, not
so much concerned if people hear, after
all it's their problem isn't it? Or
I was racing along the moon, the water's edge
seemed about right, but how was I to know
which edge? The lapping or the water? In
time it came down to these things, maybe trifles.
And sure, you can have it, "for what it's worth,"
only by that time
                    we'll have backed in again;
there's people can take these things away
as sure as others that'll bring them back to you
via the long way round. Furthermore the
boards were painted red from top to bottom.
Something like a chill elaborated a remote climate
only I wasn't talking about that, only
where the tops joined together, in a dance, weaving
together like stalks in a joyous mood open
for once.

LAUGHING CREEK

The leaves looked a little disappointed,
though they continued growing. Only angels think
they have wings. The dear future is certainly
infamous, it certainly was dangerous.

I can't remember everything in them,
these stories. She was interested in exposing
whichever things weren't going so well
the last time. Find it again by selling it.
The landlord advised trash napkins.

The brain I bring was stolen by others,
a macho dress. Others became, in their way,
his slaves, in colonies where he never saw them.
The municipality lacks water, except for the sea.
Because they don't lie to you, don't worry about it.

Daughters to be married off
before the flesh has been made bankrupt,
vehicles closer, home life, the sponsor's chair
like a hotel amusement park.
A place to do things.

And where do you find them?
Dreams? Nightmares is more like it. What's not right?
We were in Samoa. The sea will wash over us.
He came like the Johnstown flood.
It was worth waiting around for.
And the women who smiled majestically.

Give us silly, damaged things,
felony cruisers, and hours after the moon.
I lay there dumber than a dead house sparrow.
It was intentional. Snails and scales we read,
and it all ties in with Grandma, the businesses,
the absolute stench of romance. Don't even think about it.
We're very into whatever it is we're doing,
I say.

But it matters.

THE QUEEN'S APRON

Because I lack the honesty to
get up and do what I was thinking, you too
are distraught, disheveling around me so
we go out the door and are forever driven down
by a plane. Other than that needless to say
putting him into a hotel was the thing we abandoned
for a time and who's to say we will ever
contemplate our lives again. We, the unambitious.
The law hasn't happened yet while vomited sounds
ascend from the streetlight for all of us,
cake eaters, leaf-addled, who stole late things
and were pardoned because of what our relatives
on the horizon foresaw. Of course, there were lots
of accidents on the ground, but no one to sashay past
the cop on the street corner with its traffic light:
red, green, and amber, they were. Parasol, *pare-brise,*
paratonnerre. Yep it was all we thought it was, and more.
Egg floor drops. Egg ceiling follows soon after.

Where are the presumed rights we thought we were born with
I ask, and yet again: on whose farthest shore is the pine cone
torn and soon begets other lights and "issues" other

than this discriminatory paragraph I glommed in the manual.
O laborers, idle shepherds, come, a truth
I suspect once you've shifted
the blame to your flutes come undone,
I ween. No one knows how much
we've done to ourselves nor I to each other,
cracked, before we were born.

HOMELESS HEART

When I think of finishing the work, when I think of the finished work, a great sadness overtakes me, a sadness paradoxically like joy. The circumstances of doing put away, the being of it takes possession, like a tenant in a rented house. Where are you now, homeless heart? Caught in a hinge, or secreted behind drywall, like your nameless predecessors now that they have been given names? Best not to dwell on our situation, but to dwell in it is deeply refreshing. Like a sideboard covered with decanters and fruit. As a box kite is to a kite. The inside of stumbling. The way to breath. The caricature on the blackboard.

GILDERSLEEVE
ON BROADWAY

The barberries have vanished. —GEORG TRAKL

Suddenly the most dismissive sky retains
a coy aura the cellar can't fathom
or undermine. If it was spring these telltale
shards of old snow artfully scattered
beside one's path would make sense, perhaps.
As it is we're coming out into the open;
the longer one sidles, the more "him" there is
to keep the a cappella company. Yes, that's
what we would have liked back then. Stippling,
it was called. And the closer the percussionist
retreats into maculate ephemera, the wider apart
these qualities are. So tell me, why
jostle like this? Lips bleed as laughter erupts
all over the place. It told you not to come. But
since you are here, wonderfully, I'll add a comment
in the appropriate slot. Yes, you were dumb and
delightful all those years we now perceive as
patching together into a past like a "crazy"

quilt that does turn out to contain some sense
or be contained by it. Witness the runners with their poles
adding up the ridiculous glory of partial
satisfaction, the kind that gets tabled
almost immediately, to be remembered in accents and
other personal trivia long after the storm
has brooded and moved on. "Apace," you might
include. I've kept the jasmine and rotted
horseflesh separate, knowing you'll do the honors.
Destiny will greet us. After that you're on your own.

AUBURN-TINTED FENCES

No one knows the extent of the forces arrayed against us,
nor how many of them there are.

We are descended from a long line of sages, for whom it is
a point of honor not to know the quantities of things. Therein
lies our strength, alas,

and we can no more contemplate bigness than we can avoid knowledge
of the minute, that leaves a trail of goo across our sunken steps.

You who are always right about everything, come fight us. You will not
be destroyed, nor will your berm shield you from our javelins. A bear

will call with news of us. Best to be prepared to answer, but if that
isn't possible, then remember what you were taught in school. If you let
a country like this topple you, there is shelter in the long embarcations.
One afterthought is you.

Like a double chin, the glacis led down to a long commitment with the
ground. We were wearing overcoats. Nobody knew when to stop
reading or begin again, with feeling, from the top.

A sandbar led out into late afternoon. I knew I was quizzically important.
That didn't get me far, or far enough. When I think of the
motley we wore sometimes, I get all jizzed up, just for the sake of things,
or to thank somebody. And if that's all you expect in life, good, so
be it, only don't stop at the concierge's loge on your way out. *La
concierge est dans l'escalier.*

Proving that carpet sweepers were invented before vacuums.

If anybody can remember the same thing twice, we all wondered how well
we knew each other and decided to start out, though night wasn't
far off. Hell, nobody'd know if we'd arrive in time. Just take your
shoes when you leave.

THIS ECONOMY

In all my years as a pedestrian
serving juice to guests, it never occurred to me
thoughtfully to imagine how a radish feels.
She merely arrived. Half-turning
in the demented twilight, one feels a
sour empathy with all that went before.
That, needless to say, was how we elaborated
ourselves staggering across tracts:
Somewhere in America there is a naked person.

Somewhere in America adoring legions blush
in the sunset, crimson madder, and madder still.
Somewhere in America someone is trying to figure out
how to pay for this, bouncing a ball
off a wooden strut. Somewhere
in America the lonely enchanted eye each other
on a bus. It goes down Woodrow Wilson Avenue.
Somewhere in America it says you must die, you know too much.

FALSE REPORT

He fell downstream
from an adjusted height,
a side of lump.
They two, this this,
that thing. How accessible
is this? Or, mattering,
how can two care
when one is off raving,
another problem for trees
if silence is lonely?

Precarious, but not alone,
he must have remembered
wobbling like a retroactive timetable
among the tent's embers, amen.
To score its finish were
a doozy, if undeclared.
A man in a night-
gown posting the results
of better job practice
who want American products
under the doormat.

A room with six chairs
and a small table opens on
a toilet. Beyond, a view
of fields and fence posts,
beyond which a sky
good-humoredly signs in.
Wait—wasn't it
for us she did this?
Why aren't we part of the deal?
Oh, *tomorrow* night.

After the assessment
to put it mildly
like nobody's bizness
all tadpoles vanish
between the stars
and you are
nothing if not noticeable.
Won't August
grace anonymous?
I don't know!
Later, check back later
(*Popular Mechanics*). We
started at the Eiffel Tower.
A smart answer stifles a small reply.

The onyx draperies part
on a cozy octagonal scene from a car

owner's manual. It was supposed
to be something like this—
otherwise why were we summoned from the four
corners of the earth? Wait, I
think I know. It was Thanksgiving
and people were waiting for a sunset,
something to happen. Everywhere, ties
were loosened, invitations arrived
to explain the return address
inexplicably printed on the flap;
candles were tilted, bouquets
of misting fiber brought to term.

NORTHEAST BUILDING

I tell myself I'm a minimalist.
Not that it matters to the big guns
who train their sights on us,
who also know about tomorrow and their brothers,
and had a pretty good run. It would be that time
in the future, that was predicted. The wearing of boater hats
had become fairly commonplace, like going to the park.
Children ran errands while adults went to the movies.
There were more sights along the strand than at first
imagined. Nobody ever heard of an alternative
to these dingy, then bright vignettes.
We slept well and fell into an uneasy dialogue,
like the United States and Canada. Then mild everything.

The runner is already here,
has been for some time, awaiting instructions.
If it was my turn I'd go, but since that is
out of the question, I'll merely keep my counsel,
looking for some converted to preach to.
The other thing, your happiness program, fits in
with the recent trend for self-expression. All in good time.
Why is parting, then, permitted?

ELECTIVE INFINITIES

Thirsty? They race across ampersands,
scrolling. He isn't sure it's his head.
There's a delay right now. Smoke backed up.
Ladies please remove hats.

It was all over by morning. The village idiot
was surprised to see us. ". . . thought you were in Normandy."
Like all pendulums we were surprised,
then slightly miffed at what seemed to be happening
back in the bushes. Keep your ornaments,
if that's what they are. Return to sender, arse.

At the intersection a statue of a policeman
was directing traffic. It seemed like a vacation,
halloween or something. Process
was the only real thing that happened.
We wove closer to the abyss, a maze of sunflowers.
The dauphin said to take our time.

SUBURBAN BURMA

Don't try this at home. On second thought, come in,
your tumbling face ungladden. And see what happens.

The boy said, I have the look of two
through the other side of the shower. And how do we
get that, except by adding it up
in one long, fateful column.
The others are with you. Space occurs. Naturally. Not every
impulse makes it through to. You have you.
Are you a big person in the morning?

Angels of the New Year winnow followers.
We go through the motions
again. And breezes come in.
Those who remember the past are doomed to repeat it.
Plus, it's part of history.
We, however, have no such druthers.
We'll build a higher vandalism, "with the look of ending."
We were both trying to hide.

A hotel is not a big clay window
stepfathered in,
resists any effort to change the subject.
Be calm and get your stuff.

ETUDES SECOND SERIES

A cloud blew up and like
that: OK fun's fun but we've got issues,
to wait until tomorrow. At least that's
what I heard, a kind of rushing
as of water over steep slabs. More ants to fry.
I was placed on administrative leave, you
had to be there, nevertheless it sucked,
went back years. No one could find the original
copy, there were bats in the belfry.
Finally one comes down to me and says where were you.
I was only asking. Or if he had been there recently,
why there were more rafters to be removed
before you get to the roof, the actual core.
So I imagined there were infinitely more
copies like these and that we would recover
all of them. A dormer of truth sparkled.

And we were caught up, embarrassed in the shine
that hadn't meant to spear us away like that.
Parts of it were yours. When it came back
to the truth that was there, nobody could imagine
otherwise. Where once lack had been, now
was embarrassment of riches. The riches themselves
were embarrassed for what they had brought us.

So it was time to go, even if it was
that other time when nothing came in or left,
a period of ragged glare. And why not? Why shouldn't
the other trap have sprung? Its vagueness was sweet
for once. No guest could have assumed a stiffer
welcome than the one we got. The deputy was frazzled
and his sidekick hamstrung, but all came up
for the cause, there was no fighting ways about it
as long as mercenaries shuddered and satin slunk
along the shores. After all, it was the way it had
been ordered. Now I want you to just sit over there,
it's June in February and a passel o'
wild things be headin' here. If that's the case
I think I'll just be off. Oh no you don't,
you sit over there, and more's the pity.

So hours and hours were spent tapping the studs
until the requisite hollow sound whooshed forth,
making monkeys of us all. And do you think the
boy on the gourd took any notice of us? Naw, he
was too full of himself to be another's. The end
result is eponymous, like they say. If no name clings
to the door's outside you are all free to pick up
your things at the cashier's desk and mosey outward,
I suppose, if that is the kind of thing that gets recorded
hereabouts. Only let no man call the spire a skyscraper,
or angle for further farthings in the dust. Shucks,
a salesman can call that tune, honest injun, he
appropriated. It happened on a remote median, six miles from the world.

PUFF PIECE

And when I pulled it out of my pocket I thought surely
all this has been done before. And my smirched muse
answered, wholly in secret: What are apron strings
for? Your comment-clad walls feign disinterest
and sixes or sevens more, yet the petering out
of rivers will always call up terrible if tangential
echoes from foremost among us. Oh sure. And he
wants us to believe that and in how we came here. Well, Sarge,
count me out. I'm heading for a clean-named place
like Wisconsin, and mad as a jack-o'-lantern, will get there
without help and nosy proclivities. So it was on my street
the bells rang and said it was time to take an interest
in the new nuisances, wherever they might be.
                                              And I stood,
tall in the saddle, requesting information, or data,
from other echoes, and how many rascals did impeach me here,
or, of the rest of our race, implore me now
that heaven's on the line too, god or drug,
for the follow-up, because who knows when that'll be?

SAPS AT SEA

What is coffee like? Thought I'd ankle over and . . .
you know the rest. It's getting startlingly pallid
and most days are over, they portray the future
anyway. And we were so lost much of the time
it behooves understanding. The sistrums clanked aghast
as always and bees unstitched the marjoram as in the old
time and we none of us thought much about it. Winter blasts
come all too soon alas, and then what have you. Its term
by then crystallized and a clutch of unruly guests
all doing things and to each other. And who, if we were to believe
that version, might come back to upbraid us some day, not seeming
to recognize the way we all took to get here. Fame decays in a day.

I really tore something then. Then he poked me in the eye and said,
they're calling us now. Our table is ready. Did you get her answer?
I did. I was only pretending to believe as you well know
and now they're on the lookout for both of us, woe is me.
A few parishioners will try to argue
that the sinking sun is really rising. That winter
birds are part of summer's landscape. That you and I have forgotten
our separateness and are swimming together out past the horse range,
giddyap, cum frumentum. Good luck with that.
The wind blows where it wants to.
The wind will carry it away.

TANGO AND
SCHOTTISCHE

Once the grins have been harvested
and plantation themes articulated,
whatever bigwigs give you, (such as)
aloha shirts and skirts stiffened
in a classic breeze, dissolves into
our breast-feeding bill of rights.
For some bureaucrats on the ground
it's all that matters, the darker
decision. Until that's happened,
though, you want to stay offshore.
I think that Bob McCarlyle said
our region is very hot. Back in the day,
mapped homes struggled with phantom
cambrioleurs and peaceniks squealed
in every patchwork street. Once they're called in
you can adore them for what they are,
the oatmeal of contentment. I've never
seen anyone more comfortable, meaning:
You who were at Little Prong can adjudge
as long as institutional dads fumble

security and the new weather is down:
to burn and reward his sole enchantment.
That *is* what he wanted, and turned around and said,
maybe it is a good thing, the kind of face he made.

Now I remembered more than I do.
I don't plan to let anything else out.
Do not use. Give us some talc.
The four-way was conceived as a permission.
Nobody knows I'm a nudist.
Whatever stops playing is the enemy of the incomplete.

THE FOP'S TALE

The day began inauspiciously.
Well, well, I have patients who visit my family.
Silly, they don't count.
But they're alive, aren't they?
He's over here now with the invoices,
sort of cheap and busy,
fed by the scratchy wind.

They get in bed together
before going to bed
as if they needed any.
Come to the fish.

It's a good thing we weren't living in our country,
in any country, in fact, really,
if we don't go there anyway.
Now go to sleep and I'll wake you
up before the store opens.
We had a couple more walkouts,
then the coast was clear.
Isn't that a different consulate?

Who left the faucet running? By the time
it was over, thousands of hectares had been inundated.
To feed that room. He waits for me and
makes sure I am explaining the life of the mind.
Everybody makes the same children with them.
Weather tipped the guy off,
dropped the snowball.

Once there are people who died like the others,
gave up those endorsements
of selective authors,
questioned me out and
that may happen.
Pale hands I loved,
too numerous to mention.
What kind of a name is that?

A MODERN INSTANCE

In the republic of other things
when we live in a bathroom, weird issues
short out what sense orders for us.
Like a tired research assistant, you chose
to flap around, prompted by hunger, not
being sure that the crate of plums arrived.

Shoot it off the cover. A piece of the pie,
or action, will never flush early suspicions
of the nature of a cavity. There is another
problem with the census; sensory apparatus just
waiting to leave the tongue behind. The caveats,
God help 'em, were by this time so deep
in denial the servants never saw them again,
or realized they were missing. How awkward
for the heralds involved, tweeting
still through late foliage. I said you were
probably right. What more can I do?

BELLS II

For just as a misunderstanding germinates
in a clear sky, climbing like a comma
from rack to misunderstood rack of worried clouds,
now difficult, now brusque, foregrounded, amoral,
the last birds took off into the abyss.
Now it was just us, though shielded,
separate, disparate. It almost seems—
and yet it doesn't. Broken glass announces
more offenses, home invasions. Seems like
we've been here a long time. And still
ought to do those things. Every murk is a key.

No, it's all right, don't worry.
The long-fingered peninsulas have other fish to fry
as destiny germinates on summer sands, more lap top
than lap dog. And if I'd bargain you around the aisles,
don't touch it, it's a single thing.
We don't know what breviaries are mixing cocktails for us
in the V room. It's essential we be kept
out of the cordon. You should know. This is all about you:
how you arrived one cold day carrying your little knapsack
and crept in with us, to see how we could spell.
Others than old uncles hear us now,
hacking the website's early spoilage distribution plan.

FEEL FREE

Our competing lifestyles lost us the Australian double
that semester. And couldn't we then arrange
to do the other, and was the desert that limitless,
and why not say so? You see, griping comes naturally
to me and to all mankind. Once, when shut up
at the bottom of a shaft of some kind, I
assumed that the world would just trickle naturally
around whatever feet I was wearing, and increased
morbid curiosity would result. Hold on there!
No, I meant it, plangently, like small waves rubbing
against a reef, or the sighing of mice behind a grill.
This is yours to manipulate, they said,

yours to live on. That's only what they said.
I'm guessing that she told you the same,
and idlers copied it to their remotest constituency
and to a whole lot of other things, belike.

FAR HARBOR

To become lost amid underperforming texts
the stranger won't answer. By which time
it was nosebleed territory anyway. The geese
had put away their young, then fled; all that remained
to be determined was local angst, over who cares what
by sitters in a landscape. I say: how is this remote?
Yellow wine will rinse it away, and how many of us
are there? Is it my imagination or must one foregather
to bring stuff in?
                        Long before that, the tocsin
had sounded in the autumn dell. Toxins were released.
One's by-now crystallized antipathy to daring new
solutions swamped local perennial borders.

Because at least getting too serious had reputable
antecedents. Being in the way didn't matter,
nor should it, yet who knows what embarrassment can leak
this way, foreground moony entertainments? Just a clench
suffices when their guard is up. The horse pilots,
sleeping rough in their thousands,
announced commodious outcomes contradicting too-prompt

displays of local affection. The broad petals of language
are stiff and may get very bad.
They make it very bad
in our language tutoring.

THE BICAMERAL EYEBALL

No one noticed that it was midnight out.
The tools to make the tools were forthcoming.
It wasn't so much that we were afraid of farting
as that other thieves had gotten wind of his maladdress.
She was startling in her new headdress.
Oodles of trolls performed the funeral litany—
hey, it wasn't their turn at the fo'c'sle, so why
be perturbed ahead of time, and too late? The factory
whistle blew and released all the workers inside
who came crowding down along the pavement.

As though walking on stilts people blew up in amazement
like pieces of trash a wind desultorily lifts,
then returns for no visible reason. We were all tired
and happy, plodders on life's great thoroughfare.
None of us were in it for the long haul, but paradoxically
all of us were, we just didn't know it yet. But when I
looked over at her I could see why they meant sadness,
not from any bereavement, but growing like a stem
in otherwise barren ground. Oh, sure, there was plenty of majolica
on buffets in those days, chafing dishes with lids
to be lifted and then put back again. There were mild

pools in the woods far from any stream, and ant-size
buggies patrolling the slopes. Good thing for you
it was too. That they were there. Or just on the threshold
of being, like a dream. I told you not to be a gnat
about things, that sooner or later worrying would grow up
to become part of experience. It was just that you
seemed to believe me when I wasn't being especially serious.

That, and the tens of revolutions to come. I say,
shall we go inside? The combination of rain and sunshine
always finds me defeated, and then other causes come along,
seeking attribution. Meanwhile if he matriculates
in one to ten years, who's to say I'm not stodgy either?
It was all we could do, her and I, to keep from laughing
at his strife. Meanwhile the fire burned bright.
The maids grew petulant.
But I don't care, really, none of us could
as long as time brings up the rear, placing a napkin,
folded just so, over the era and whatever it
thought it was up to. Now, doesn't that make a lot of sense?

POEM BEGINNING WITH A LINE FROM <u>GAMMER GURTON'S NEEDLE</u>

When Diccon the Bedlam had heard by report
about the basting, and sensible replies to it
from people here and there, think first of those
looking very worried, and that will be an end to it.
Yes, and farther along the path to school
were mutterings: Some claimed the end of the world
had come, others that it was fast approaching.
Finally no one knew that anything was going on
for long, and kept their thoughts to themselves:
Why, Gammer, we had no idea something was lost
and that you had lost it, pray? *I'll teach ya a lesson.*
And night flowed into the pond as though it were a lagoon.

They knew, and were interested.
Little events in the house drew the attention
but not for long, and it was as though rose leaves
on the paper were really leaves. There's no time
to keep this, not too much anyway. There's time

you were owed, and the time you owned, and between them
the match that was called. You slid down
into a chair and it was like so much that happens
every day and no one is wiser for it, nor wiser
before it happened, on someone's day off:
Cashier the jerks, kiss the bald head
and we'll be on our way, not being proud
nor ashamed either. That would be it.

NOT BEYOND
ALL CONJECTURE

Oblivion scattereth her poppy, and besides,
it's time to go inside now,
feed the aggressive pets, forgive our trespasses
for trespassing against us.
                              Other times
monotony is like a cave, the air is fresh,
tedium tonic.
                   We live in a museum of helpful objects,
leaning toward the accomplishment of a small,
complicated task, like sailors in rigging.
Something no American has yet achieved.

INSTEAD OF LOSING

Anyone, growing up in a space you hadn't used yet
would've done the same: bother the family's bickering
to head straight into the channel. My, those times
crackled near about us, from sickly melodrama
instead of losing, and the odd confusion . . . confusion.

I thought of it then, and in the mountains.
During the day we perforated the eponymous city limits
and then some. No one knew all about us
but some knew plenty. It was time to leave that town
for an empty drawer
into which they sailed. Some of the eleven thousand
virgins were getting queasy. I say, stop the ship!
No can do. Here come the bald arbiters
with their eyes on chains, just so, like glasses.
Heck, it's only a muskrat
that's seen better years, when things were medieval
and gold . . .

So you people in the front,
leave. You see them. And you understand it all.
It doesn't end, night's sorcery notwithstanding.

Would you have preferred to be a grown-up in earlier times
than the child can contain or imagine?
Or is right now the answer—you know, the radio
we heard news on late at night,
our checkered fortunes so lucky.
Here's your ton of plumes, and your Red Seal Records.
The whole embrace.

LAUNDRY LIST

The stranger walks toward the children, who walk
into the sky. A lesson is born. There are those
who'll say we're better for it. Not us, though.
We were born to ignore warning signs and deny witness tampering.
Otherwise we'll keep to the agenda forged for us.
Tinned elegies. "That" pretty much encapsulates it
while our time on the planet ambiguously finishes.

And though we were nominated for honors,
others ascended in our place, were silent
in the enveloping paradox. Invited to inspect old cars,
few realized what he or she was assenting to,
nor how a blank wall turned state's evidence bloomed
into a parlor of paranormal events and happenings—
just what we'd expected of the leafless afternoon's bestirring twitch.

"Most storied"—I'm getting there
though I don't need the attention—hardly,
because it just happens, or . . . ?

I don't know how I feel.
It's ignorance of numbers and their consequences, us too.
Propped on an ambiguous plaid in a cottage orné, one listens

to forgotten arias from a petunia-shaped speaker.
Donna è mobile. Où va la jeune Hindoue?
Oui, c'est elle, c'est la déesse. But don't
release me just yet. Too little is too soon.
As well groan like a paddleboat in a ditch
as come to accept these late practices as our own.
Many questions remain

                and want no part in it.

PALMY

Not beaten to a pulp, not even tapped
on the shoulder in the crowd at noon
by a well-meaning but careless friend,
then left to sink under your own regard.
So what if children don't dance, and burghers
recall their dignitas? It was your scruples
brought us here. I first read you that.
The time to go home has been now.

He will have thickened, your vast friend,
always sentient for what their agents
might deploy, then barren, less hybrid, sustained
by a mood. Shadows replace what looked
dappled then, when there were fewer takers,
more points of origin, less evaluation. More brass,
less hubris. It all balances out in the opposite
current that keeps us alive, the baleful
and the artless. Fathers, sons, accountants, cars
asked us to keep their place. We grew innocent.

YOU WHAT?

Serious eaters from here to Kankakee welcome
the disaggregation of religion into irreducible
chips, dot dot dot. Carsick in Canada you can
feel it coming up. You can feel it coming.
Something will turn up. You'll notice something
going on, nasty impact, a bit chewed under.
How modern we were! For people in high school
across the region of the Canadian peninsula,
that's when we activate the bases. How he got into
the apartment is anyone's guess, and no one's.
Shooting stars dodge the Hubble's perimeter.
Nobody tells dogs how to behave, people either.
What's needed is a priest, or lacking that a raincoat.
Let's all be in a fuzzy argument.
It comes to some fanciful verbal frottage or tegument.
Times sure were bleak then but we loved a ragged stranger.

SILENT AUCTION

A sundial in the *jardin des supplices*
indicates a convenient, if makeshift, hideaway,

just what we were looking for
in the time of our engagement.

Grosgrain flutters from a corncrib.
The sheep are all past.

When I went for a walk it seemed
as though the whole city was there,

confined in trombone-like tubes.
One salesman asked me to please hold thy neighbor;

another, if brightness was indeed falling.
I answered as best I knew, telling him

to look it up in an old phone directory.
Not twenty pages later I passed the woman

who knew this was a lie, but bravely
took it on the chin for me. Some women are great!

My first is a lanky stuffed gorilla.
I did all these things in the past.

Whole embassies have crashed, and now, thank you,
the measurable pain is coming due.

We who segued on the sidelines,
unfelt-up and driven, know how it aches

and keep our peace. Wow, kitty, that sure
looked real, you've got to admit, and I in my wrapper

and Mama in her cap put out stories about the new
mood that slurped above the horizon,

the *Tannhäuser* lost in the local *mer des glaces,*
for once unsung, though thoroughly inebriated.

CARD OF THANKS

Asked if he liked mutton, he turned away. No,
not here, this is today! And others might have it so.
He galloped away like a sheep, who seldom lacked champions
in his young time, when bored they came and sat beside him
in twilight sometimes, and violet rocks ceased chanting
about the sublime to organize later façades
of marsh gas. O it seemed subtle, whatever was hissing
like a vulture over the town. You're going to feel well,
giants of rhetoric, devastating in the now.

Nominated for the likely reimbursement, who are
we to argue across the shirt, or pressure, which is wrong,
two flatfoots and an even bigger sea?

Whatever, I'm
grateful for this moment of trying, criminal tuberose,
only it was so unlike me I
started to cry in the van. Somebody picked up on
me being included at all. What's your
status? Oh, I came along with the others,
was sorted out and blotted in with them when times

were dense and nobody knew when the future would be. O
let's dream inside each other, should be.
My furniture ball makes a wand when unstrutted;
two cameos vie for three listings.
The beautiful disease catches us all.

MARIVAUDAGE

We are all patting sleeping shoes
on a string. The board of selection
takes precedence at such times as arise
in the sky broken conduits and stresses
and as such may be over, this time.
Pass the Durkee's. And repent.

Yes sir it shall be done unto you
as the maze requests, fiber inspected
and the president is eight months old.
To come in with a lid to the physical area
though bordered by tracts, is as a great
expression unto these untimely limbs.
This *is* what he wanted. Maybe it is a good thing
for some people, not those present, and turned
around and said, what is it to your gaming
and japes, the bald-colored
fiber of daily life in the offing, to which
he replied only that the seam shapes itself
in building up to some calm, inconceivable commentary.

MARINE SHADOW

Just being washed out to sea, bashed around—
this impression, I mean this what you hear
is part of it. And quite useless. We're talking
non-fiction, which pours through at lunch time,
the whole stinking phenomenology wound into it
at the base of the stalk. From there it branches
out into other axioms and metaphors. Like,
I have a brand in Chicago. You'd better think about it.

Action figures take us just so far, to the edge
of the abyss. The fucking man swears by rifles.
The sparrow boys agreed. Everywhere that Mary went
dynasties collapsed amid gnashing teeth, and soon other
solvents reached the opposite shore, but this was only a test.
Time enough for the purple brine of consequences,
the tumbling package of breakers released by the breeze.
Cue bugle and castanets. This being more of an occasion
than that. It promised shy retribution. It's listing,
bungled. It can't, can it?

"BEYOND ALBANY
AND SYRACUSE . . ."

As handwriting sprawls
a page, revealing much about the writer's psyche,
so too these lemons, dividends
of peace, in our time, my friend.

Don't stagger the bejesus out of the old harness,
play with the dog, who yaps
afresh at any pretext of the blond air,
or stifle the air's partisans, the moments.

Hard to pin down when the motorcade
stopped before your house.
Handsome, or stupid, got out, the brass oak leaves
draped over his forearm. "Methinks . . ."

That such a day existed, in gullies
and canyons, down to the picture
of this very day, fresh as a haircut,
puzzles minds. The year may not remember
the hurt, but the hurt does,

hidden among lobes of the augur plant
or phrasing in the sky. Blown off course,
but the course remains, faded watermark,
shadow of all resilience, to be found once summer
has ended, a random sarcophagus
viewed from the hotel kitchens.
Tree that sheltered Grandmother.
And you are it.

To have life come in at 70¢ less,
awful venal perverted life . . .
They must have started by now,
the manipulative strands.

We don't need to do it yet,
not let a little thing like breathing handicap us.
Look at boxcars, at weapons in general.
Thunderstorms collected on the bridge.
A young nonprofessional tried to add it up.
Always there was more, yet somehow fewer
entities among the gaps in categories.

But then, these are quite different.

NEVER TWO
WITHOUT THREE

Seeing through glasses what the glasses put there
or wanted to see, one opts out. They have seen
and too clearly what runners-up have been accused
too thoroughly of seeing, and that's it,
for the one time. Optimum runners, jadeite blinkers.
What was that I meant, or said? Alas, it had no style,
was shifted by a library trustee, let fall where it
casually was, the audience "none the wiser."

Otherwise there's not much to get excited about.
Tears fall in place in the classroom, it having been decided
to look elsewhere on this day, and all will
end kindly, abruptly, the way things ended
when you read about them and longed to see how
they were coming along, just once, in this orchard
of the truth no one believes in, and has the country been affected.
That's only what they said, or something.

A loud noise will contradict silence every time.
Memory is so busy, retrieving orbs thought glistery

in their day, now a source of indignation.
Perhaps that's why the contest rules stressed sincerity,
neatness, and aptness of thought. Who else
would be looking out for one, after all, at this late date?
It's a backward odyssey, ending at the poisoned spring,
with nothing, ever, to be done about it, or blame apportioned
in old newspapers blown across blue
pavement into chain-link fence, sad to see us go.

MABUSE'S
AFTERNOON

That's a map of Paris on the fender,
if that's a fender. Passy, the 63 bus,
the thirteenth arrondissement, are on it.
It says, do something, do *something*,
even if it's for yourself. Hey,
that's an idea. It can come closer
without ever getting close enough.

All the times in the last week
are storied doom. Paris seemed
to initiate a conversation. Others intervened.
Oh my, they said. *Oh* my. That's just it,
you can't have it only one way. You like
eggs with that? Oh I'm only going about
my business. What business? Well,
if you say so. Fall down the street.

Gentlemen thank you very much.
We're here for a middle reception
that shall raise us up

one of those businesses where you came to mind
very much.
The opposite was horses kicking,
beautiful shadow grooves that illustrate
how this was meant to be
in time
and other systems fell in line,
creating themselves and the dim aura
that projected them. For sure we only noticed it
had gone when it came back again
for a little while and weren't sure we'd noticed it.
Hands wove round us like gloves
that supported us and weren't too sure
who was doing the supporting.
I can hear them and many sides.

I don't think it has nothing to do with it,
it kind of stood out,
balanced on my hair.
You've salvaged those oxen.
Conditions still intrude, gases
won't savage you all at once, trying to be
nice as usual and taking flak for it,
guiding rookies or young people who may one day traipse.
A little light rain goes up
faster, he said; then: It vanished.

THE RETURN OF
FRANK JAMES

Not me dreaming, only the predictable
backwash of shells, stones. A harp that once
but otherwise knew no fringed paths,
why it's everywhere. And when we wanted it,
went to look for it, any ghost was there.

Only riding around sometimes the miserable
retreat raffles off some joy or other.
Then maidens beat each other to the spring.
It was all on time's account, ye were daft
to speculate otherwise. That's why I know you're there.
You want me to put my fortune on hold and not tether
time's likeliest assent to what we were there doing,
asleep, holding each other the holiest way.
That was a parade of not doing, thanks.
You mean you want me to put my oar in the shaft.

Ack you mean you, going out into this weather,
him but a chicken inspector
and we all are united with our claims at the end

of a suitcase filled with bizarre retention?
(One of his more obscure vehicles.)

Woman right behind you prompted celebrity
and aardvark/hosiery task force underneath.
We decided to clock in. Nice headline.
Ack you mean you
you want me to put my
where and when's customs
and one-of-a-kind advice.
You actually noticed.
By that time others were set to go,
dreams, perfumes, the sheriff's pants
stiffened on a hedge for all the world lifelike.
Minus vibrato. Ponying up, shaken,
released into one's custody.
Just a few dreams and such.

FIVE O'CLOCK SHADOW

Whence I came is
"very different," looks pretty,
balkanized already.

Things bother you along.
It's so interesting when
the beautiful things on the table
listen, in a trance.

What's an afternoon among friends?
What can you do?

THE FUTURE
OF THE DANCE

Who do we go to?
Depending on who they are, children
work in the fields. Vacation is coming
and they expect life will go on like this
for several mornings in a row. Hurry, sewing machine,
the quicker to accomplish what is expected of you.
Fish leap partly out of the water. And the air is new.

Earlier, illustrious strangers accosted us
(depending on who they are), bade us sit
and listen as though to a tale. And in the sky,
collapsing fountains watered our feet
as their long-winded account lubricated the airs
and vines that stirred in them then.
No one expects life to be a single adventure,
yet conversely, one is surprised when it turns disappointing,
as tales so often do when the telling doth outpace
the situation. Hurry up and sleep,
I suggest. And if that prove lonely,
the song will not have gone for naught.

Painted groves do more for prowess
than terraces and minarets. Bicycles revive
the landscapes they are scoring. Better a silent
accordion than a chorus of harps, be they this way
or that other, crying crystal drops
that hang about once evening has made its weather.
Blander scenes were always the ones farther away,
but these leaves that curled in our hands,
fig and nettle, survive in a notch of time
clocks cannot undo, nor fortune despoliate.

WITHAL

Or in other, partial, hearings a slant away
until they can, tally the activated result
as it would have happened moon mountains ago.
Say, is there anything wrong with sitting around
capably, like this, one shin tucked in?
The others wait for you to do their shy bidding,
like kids, once. The turmeric sky concurred
in the adagio of the afterfright, just like this!
There were of course other factors to be bargained in,
but in the end it made no cause, we were up and corseted
and the behind principals mattered not. Oh, but
this was some kind of a school. Air shoved lessons
in and out of it, neutral, adhesive, like a school
of fish seen only one time. Litigation intruded:
What were the facts to be classified now? Zillions,
I'd wager. And over and behind it all the old shade,
as deleted as a Chinese risk factor. Oh, say,
all along the way it turned into light. Was supple.

Without that carbonated fizz his self-deprecating
gambit fell into shards like patterned shawls, are to this day.

IPHIGENIA
IN SODUS

Why does that name sound so familiar?
If I were you I shouldn't worry, or ask.

But—isn't that collusion?
Well, yes, technically it is,

but we're a long way from truth here.
Well, it all *seems* right, but we'll have to

put different bodies on the gentlemen—
Something that speaks to truth, as she is now,

which is how we all had envisioned her:
wrapped in jade strips, more or less flyblown,

somewhat sloppy about the mouth these days.
Excuse me, I had issues,

but then the doors sagged, the window frames
had disappeared a long time ago into the murk

of this age. Seen now, she pivots frantically
near where we—they—arrive to consult the oracle,

making small talk the while, about how whose
elections needed shortening, and how all this

streamed away into cozier times, in ways kind to me,
before chopping them down.

BACON GRABBERS

Once when it was full summer and I was remembering
what it was like coming to get you across fields in a dress
the full meaning or breathing revealed itself to me
and I was like a child seated beside a stream, O dismal!
The pairings went on, and the partings. And who, if we were
to believe this version, might accommodate her own paisley truth?
You could say, "It stinks," but the mirror tells another story,
freckled, noted, wisps of ash traveling in all rightness
to defend the mob, all day in the streets' shifting gutters,
alien to truth's slobber. We hatched a magnificent ovenload
of furies for that time, nobody could figure out what we were
doing so it mattered even less. Other times, *au clair de la lune* each
peach blow seemed to appeal if he . . . then you should go,
helping themselves to it and all should be well, yea even as I
direct you to find a place the sisters parade untaxed,
no Mormons over the hill. Helping themselves to it limitless
a jungle spree erupts, a maddeningly slow landslide chirps
beside the counterpane and all is mostly lost.

I figured

that out easily and made extra time too, nobody that day
was as reliant as me. Forty more sawbucks crested,

and that was only a précis. If not, the seven maids
and seven spades must sign for it. I'll be out in the territory.
I had to go to my sister-in-law's for the long weekend.
Does her address seem relevant? We had a laughing machine
in the basement . . .

VIEWERS
WILL RECALL

We gathered the threads into an equation.
Here it was dark and violet. There a service road
led smoothly into the highway. It was understood
that our "culture of complaint" would bear
the blame for the time being. That the high-rise
was a symbol for God.

In-between times were different, and the same.
The mirror was like a French movie.
Guests greeted each other and went out
into a vacancy of clouds and vehicles.
Why were none of them here before me?
Who's counting? A private leaf chided
the whole darn infrastructure, kept us from moving
even as we sailed away on wings of tether.

Now would be a good time to counsel strangers
about improved coverage, the mote
on the garage floor, dances that know no other way
yet keep backing into this one. The alternative
wasn't so nice either.

A lucky thing we knew no other:
Sniffing away at the barrier, at twos and sixes,
one gradually became accustomed to the loss of light:
The young ones who came up to sit with us awhile were gone.
In their place were only trees, trees as roosts.
A few more minutes and it will be over again.
Stop it, you're listening to me.

POSTLUDE AND PREQUEL

Would I lie to you? I don't know what to say to you,
and the season is coming into season just now
with long-awaited words from back when we were
friends and still are, of course, but the tides
pursue their course each day. Perturbing elements
listen in the wings, which are coming apart at the seams.
Is it all doggerel and folderol? A cracked knowledge?
Monkey journalism?

This is better than the other overlooked good
that dried up a while back and whispers.
The results, if any, won't last too much longer
and I meanwhile am on my way to correct you
about the tickets and their availability.
We pitch and stiffen, elbowed by traffic mysteriously
descending the other lane of the avenue
as lamps burst in many-benched Central Park.

[UNTITLED]

Can we start again?
The messenger is waiting for a reply,
but there is none, only a tattoo
from the cloud motet, signifying
the waiting has ended. This is the argument,
shuffling into afternoon, and with luck,
on into evening, in whose mirror it will recognize itself.
Would you bring that next week?
Otherwise, fear the clipped lawns,
speckled with birdhouses, noncommittal shrubbery.
It was always supposed to be like this.
Night and day were equally at fault,
childhood was let off the hook. There are no words to
erect the prison whose walls are locking in place,
a haunted bower, not at all disagreeable,
only singular. The pillars, the parquet embroidered it
into permanence. We needed that.

The author gratefully acknowledges the following publications in which poems in *Quick Question* first appeared, sometimes in slightly different form: *American Poetry Review, The American Scholar, Australian Book Review, The Believer, Boston Review, Conjunctions, Half Circle, Harper's, jubilat, London Review of Books, Maggy, The Massachusetts Review, The New Republic, The New York Review of Books, The New Yorker, Notre Dame Review, The Paris Review, PEN America, PN Review, Sentence: A Journal of Prose Poetics, This Corner, The Times Literary Supplement,* and *Wave Composition.*

"The Allegations," "Bacon Grabbers," "Cross Island," "In a Lonely Place," "The New Crowd," "Rest Area," "Saps at Sea," "Unlike the Camelopard," and "[untitled]" were first published in the chapbook *Three Poets* with work by Timothy Donnelly and Geoffrey G. O'Brien (Minus A Press).

"Beyond Albany and Syracuse . . . ," "Mabuse's Afternoon," and "Withal" were published in *In/Filtration: An Anthology of Hudson Valley Innovative Poetics* (Station Hill).

"Instead of Losing" first appeared in the Academy of American Poets' "Poem-A-Day" e-mail series.

"Marine Shadow" was first published in the Institute of Contemporary Art/Boston's catalogue for the exhibit *Figuring Color: Kathy Butterly, Felix Gonzalez-Torres, Roy McMakin, Sue Williams,* edited by Jeremy Sigler.

"Palmy" was first published as the Poetry Collection's 2011 Holiday Broadside by the University at Buffalo Libraries (SUNY).

"Words to That Effect" first appeared in *Harold Bloom: 80*, a birthday festschrift printed by *The Yale Review*, and was included in *Gods and Tramps: An Anthology of Poets and Poems* by photographer Jemimah Kuhfeld.

"Five O'Clock Shadow" first appeared in a book of tributes to Bill Berkson (Brooklyn Rail).

"A Voice from the Fireplace" was published as a broadside in Australia (Polar Bear Press).

On the following pages, a stanza break occurs at the bottom of the page (not including pages on which the break is evident because of the regular stanzaic structure of the poem): 16, 29, 45, 48, 60, 93, 100.

JOHN ASHBERY was born in Rochester, New York, in

1927. He earned degrees from Harvard and Columbia, and went to France as a Fulbright Scholar in 1955, living there for much of the next decade. His many collections of poetry include *Planisphere* (2009) and *Notes from the Air: Selected Later Poems* (2007), which was awarded the 2008 International Griffin Poetry Prize. *Self-Portrait in a Convex Mirror* (1975) won the three major American prizes—the Pulitzer, the National Book Award, and the National Book Critics Circle Award—and an early book, *Some Trees* (1956), was selected by W. H. Auden for the Yale Younger Poets Series. The Library of America published the first volume of his collected poems in 2008. He has published numerous translations from the French, including works by Pierre Reverdy, Arthur Rimbaud, Raymond Roussel, and several collections of poems by Pierre Martory. Active in various areas of the arts throughout his career, he has served as executive editor of *Art News* and as art critic for *New York* magazine and *Newsweek*; he exhibits his collages at the Tibor de Nagy Gallery (New York). He taught for many years at Brooklyn College (CUNY) and Bard College, and in 1989–90 delivered the Charles Eliot Norton lectures at Harvard. He is a member of the American Academy of Arts and Letters (receiving its Gold Medal for Poetry in 1997) and the American Academy of Arts and Sciences, and was a chancellor of the Academy of American Poets from 1988 to 1999. The winner of many prizes and awards, both nationally and internationally, he has received two Guggenheim Fellowships and was a MacArthur Fellow from 1985 to 1990; most recently, he received the Medal for Distinguished Contribution to American Letters from the National Book Foundation (2011) and a National Humanities Medal, presented by President Obama at the White House (2012). His work has been translated into more than twenty-five languages. He lives in New York. Additional information is available in the "About John Ashbery" section of the Ashbery Resource Center's website, a project of The Flow Chart Foundation, www.flowchartfoundation.org/arc.

N?